GRAYSLAKE AREA PUBLIC LIBRARY

3 6109 00537 4423

P9-DDT-046

NO LONGER OWNED BY
GRAYSLAKE PUBLIC LIBRARY

Mind Games

LEFT BRAIN, RIGHT BRAIN

Facts, Trivia, and Quizzes

creative

logic

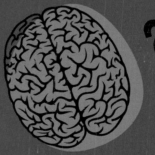

Francesca Potts

Lerner Publications ◆ Minneapolis

GRAYSLAKE AREA PUBLIC LIBRARY
100 Library Lane
Grayslake, IL 60030

Copyright © 2018 by Lerner Publishing Group, Inc.

All rights reserved. International copyright secured. No part of this book may be reproduced, stored in a retrieval system, or transmitted in any form or by any means—electronic, mechanical, photocopying, recording, or otherwise—without the prior written permission of Lerner Publishing Group, Inc., except for the inclusion of brief quotations in an acknowledged review.

Lerner Publications Company
A division of Lerner Publishing Group, Inc.
241 First Avenue North
Minneapolis, MN 55401 USA

For reading levels and more information, look up this title at www.lernerbooks.com.

Main body text set in Avenir LT Pro
Typeface provided by Linotype

Library of Congress Cataloging-in-Publication Data

The Cataloging-in-Publication Data for *Left Brain, Right Brain* is on file at the Library of Congress.
ISBN 978-1-5124-3414-9 (lib. bdg.)
ISBN 978-1-5124-4940-2 (EB pdf)

Manufactured in the United States of America
1-42050-23920-2/20/2017

3 6109 00537 4423

Y
153
POT
3.18 dz

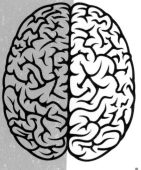

CONTENTS

Introduction
BRAIN BATTLE

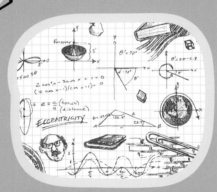

You're back at school after staying home sick yesterday. To catch up, you borrow notes from your friends Sam and Erin. Sam's notes are super organized with neat lists. The ideas in Erin's notes are connected with swirly arrows. Doodles fill the page.

It's obvious that your friends do not take in data the same way. It's almost as if their brains work differently!

intuition

HALF-BRAINED?

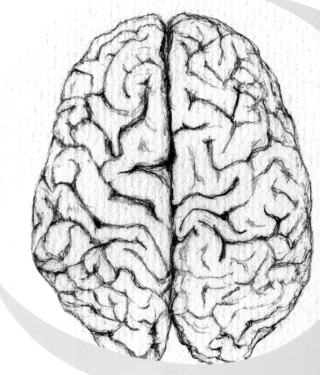

In the past, some scientists believed people used one side of their brain more than the other. Each side was linked with certain functions or **traits**. They thought right-brained people were **creative** and emotional. And they believed left-brained people were more **rational** and **logical**.

Scientists now know that this theory is false. People use both sides of their brain equally! But the theory is based on the ways people make decisions and learn. And it can be a great way to learn more about yourself!

Chapter 1
BRAIN BELIEFS

People have been interested in the brain and how it works since ancient times. As early as 1700 BCE, ancient Egyptians wrote of its **anatomy**. People weren't sure exactly what the brain's purpose was.

MIND BIND

In the 1960s, scientist Roger Wolcott Sperry knew that the brain is divided into two sections called hemispheres. But he discovered that either hemisphere can continue to function even if the other half does not! Sperry also confirmed that different areas of the brain control different functions. For example, speech processing takes place in a different hemisphere of the brain than processing art or music.

creative

It's True!

Your brain hemispheres control your body movements. But they do this in a crisscross fashion! The right brain controls the movement of the left side of your body. The left brain controls the movement of the right side of your body.

DISTORTING DATA

The public was excited about Sperry's brain hemisphere discoveries. However, many misinterpreted it. People began to believe that a person's personality was determined by which hemisphere was dominant in their brain.

LEFT AND RIGHT

The left brain oversees logic, organization, and rational thought.
The right brain oversees emotions and creative thinking.

People who identify with functions that take place in the left brain called themselves left-brained. Those who identify more with the functions that take place in the right brain called themselves right-brained.

Are You Left-Brained or Right-Brained?

Even though theories of being left-brained or right-brained were proven false, they are still fun to think about! Answer the questions below. Follow the path with your finger. Find out if you are left-brained, right-brained, or both!

Is your room usually clean?

yes — Do you wear a watch, or are you always on time?

no — Do you keep a diary or journal of stories?

yes — Do math and science come naturally to you?

no — Do you think you could be **hypnotized**?

no — Do you keep a diary or journal of stories?

yes — Is art, music, or creative writing your favorite subject in school?

yes — Do you prefer to read nonfiction books that contain a lot of facts and data?

no — Do you need complete silence to study?

no — Is art, music, or creative writing your favorite subject in school?

yes — Do you prefer to read mystery or **fantasy** novels?

yes — You are left-brained!

no — You are both left-brained and right-brained!

no — You are right-brained!

9

Chapter 2

ALL ABOUT THE RIGHT BRAIN

Are you artistic, thoughtful, and emotional? Do you love music? Then you might consider yourself right-brained! The right side of the brain is a center of creativity.

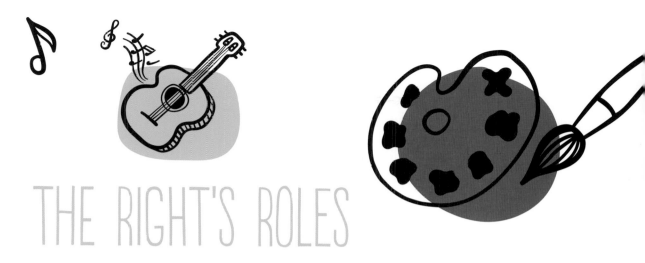

THE RIGHT'S ROLES

Your right brain helps you identify 3-D shapes and people's faces. It is responsible for your awareness of music and art.

People who identify as right-brained can sometimes be emotional and sensitive to others' feelings. They are often creative. But they can sometimes be disorganized!

THE RIGHT JOB

People who identify as right-brained often work in artistic fields. They may become singers, designers, or artists. But remember, these people also use the left sides of their brains! Your brain can take on any career you choose.

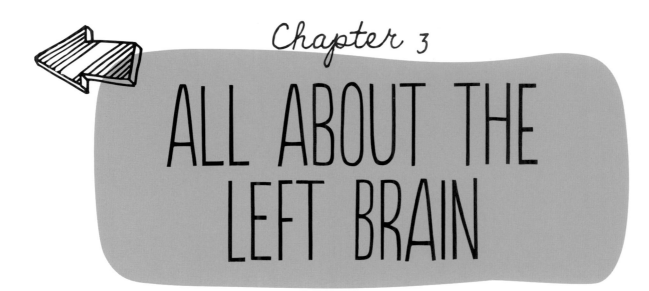

Chapter 3

ALL ABOUT THE LEFT BRAIN

Do you like to analyze things? Do you like to do puzzles, crosswords, or other brain games? Then you might consider yourself left-brained! The left side of your brain functions in logic.

HANG LEFT

Your left brain controls language, mathematics, and computing. It also goes into action when you memorize something.

People who identify as left-brained are often very organized. They like to have a **routine** and enjoy planning ahead and problem-solving. They **evaluate** details to create a concrete solution.

LEFT FIELDS

Left-brained people often find jobs in science, **technical**, or detail-oriented fields. They may become engineers, doctors, or computer programmers. But even if you identify as left-brained, you can still do any job you set your mind to!

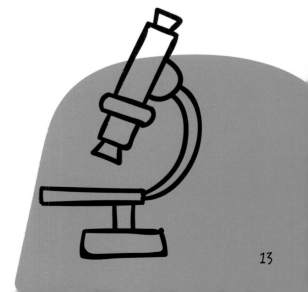

Chapter 4

WORK IT OUT!

Did you decide if you are left-brained or right-brained? Whichever hemisphere you identify with, it does not mean the other side is asleep. It is important to exercise all parts of your brain.

BUILDING BRAIN MUSCLE

If you lift weights, your muscles get stronger. The same is true with your brain! If you find you identify more with one brain hemisphere, you can work out the other to make it stronger.

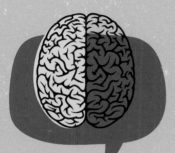

LEFT-BRAIN WORKOUTS

Activating your brain's left hemisphere takes activities that involve logic. Completing puzzles is a good left-brain workout. This includes crosswords and math puzzles, such as Sudoku. Learning a new language and word games also **ignite** the left side of the brain.

MAKE IT RIGHT

Do you feel that you identify more with functions in your left brain hemisphere? Then there are lots of fun activities you can do to ignite the right side. Get ready to think outside the box!

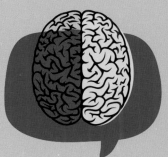

RIGHT-BRAIN WORKOUTS

Doing activities that use your imagination will help you exercise your right brain. These could include drawing, painting, and writing poems. If you want to really activate your right brain, try to draw a picture using your non-dominant hand!

Musical activities are also a great right-brain workout. Try singing, playing an instrument, or making up a new song.

It's True!

Translating language is an activity that uses both your right and left brain. Your left brain translates each word. Your right brain puts everything together to see the big picture and gather meaning.

hola

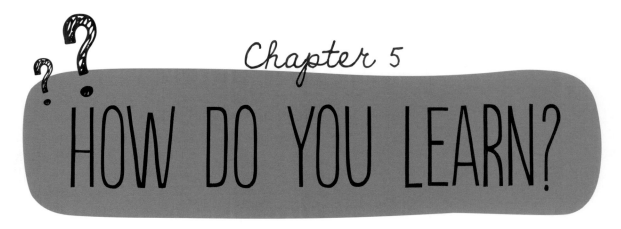

Chapter 5
HOW DO YOU LEARN?

Being right-brained or left-brained can greatly affect your learning style. There are many ways to take in information.

RIGHT-BRAIN REQUIREMENTS

If you are right-brained, you learn best by doing an activity instead of reading about it. You ask open-ended questions and you shine when working in a group with lots of discussion and **brainstorming**. However, listening to instructions can be difficult for you. You might find yourself doodling during lectures.

creative

LEFT-BRAINED LEARNING

Left-brain learners often do very well in traditional school settings. If you are left-brained, you are very focused on details and facts. You learn best through reading and listening. Left-brained thinkers are usually most **productive** when they work alone. They prefer quiet spaces for studying. They use organized notes and lists to remember facts and concepts.

logic

LEARNING LEFT

If you identify as right-brained, traditional classroom settings can be a challenge. But you can adapt! Create visuals like pictures or cartoons to help you understand information. Or turn the information into a song to help you remember facts.

THINKING RIGHT

If you identify as left-brained, try these tricks to help you learn more creative tasks. Keep a pencil and paper nearby when processing art and music. Write down the rules of music or facts about works of art. This organizing of data may help you perform right-brained tasks more easily!

What's Your Learning Style?

You might consider yourself left-brained or right-brained. But your learning style may not fit your brain type! Answer the questions below. Write down your answers on a separate sheet of paper. Tally your results to discover how you best learn new things.

1. What types of books do you enjoy the most?

A. the more pictures, the better

B. audiobooks

C. books with words, no pictures

D. activity books, like those with puzzles or quizzes

2. You're at summer camp and want to learn a new skill. This could be sailing, swimming, or knitting. How do you prefer to be taught?

A. watch a **demonstration**

B. listen to someone tell you what to do

C. read instructions

D. jump in and learn as you go

3. You go to a birthday party for your best friend. What will you remember most?

A. who was there and what they were wearing

B. the music that played in the background

C. the invitation or the birthday banner

D. yourself dancing and eating all the birthday treats

4. What is your favorite subject in school?

A. art

B. music

C. math or science

D. gym

5. How do you prefer to relax?

A. watching your favorite TV show

B. listening to music

C. getting lost in a great book

D. playing sports or going for a run

ANSWERS:

Mostly As: Visual Learner
You prefer using pictures and **diagrams** to understand information.

Mostly Bs: Audio Learner
You learn best when you hear information. This can include music and speech.

Mostly Cs: Verbal Learner
Reading or writing is how you learn best.

Mostly Ds: Tactile Learner
You learn best when taking a hands-on approach, such as drawing and building.

Chapter 6

DECISION DESIGN

Try to remember the last decision you made. Do you have it?
Even the act of settling on the memory was a decision!
Your brain makes decisions all day long. Some decisions
require a lot of thinking. Others are almost
automatic. Your left and right brain
are always ready to divide duties
to help you make decisions.

WHAT TO DO?

Imagine that you want to be on the school's baseball team this spring. But you love to act and want to do the spring play! Practices for both activities are at the same time each week. You must choose which to take part in. How do you decide?

TO THE FRONT!

All decision-making takes place in the frontal lobe. This is a part of the brain that spans both hemispheres.

intuition

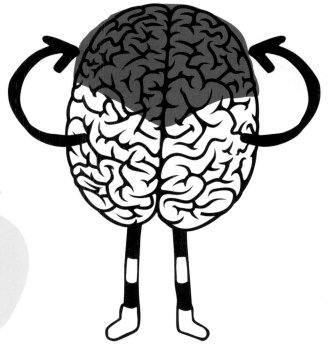

emotion

FACTS OR FEELINGS?

Left-brained individuals make decisions using data and logic. They often place more importance on common sense than emotions. They focus on facts to make a decision.

Right-brained thinkers often focus on emotions to make decisions. They may make decisions based on how they feel. They often rely on a gut feeling instead of common sense.

BALANCING ACT

Research has shown that the best decisions are made using *both* sides of your brain! Next time you need to decide something, try using methods you've never used before. Did it affect your decision?

Do You Make Decisions Based on Emotion or Logic?

Do you use your head or your heart to make decisions? Read the statements below. If you agree with a statement, give yourself one point. Tally your points on a separate sheet of paper.

Part 1:

- Your favorite types of movies have a happy storyline.

- When you argue with someone, your heart starts racing. You might even scream and yell.

- You are very kind and caring. You open your heart to everyone, including animals!

- You love learning about people and their behaviors.

- You think about how your decisions will affect others. You feel bad when people's feelings are hurt.

Part 2:

- Your friend asks your opinion about something. You give the honest answer even though it may not be what they want to hear.

- You always follow the rules.

- Your favorite types of books are about history or science.

- You believe there is always a right or a wrong answer.

- You enjoy research and learning facts.

Add up your points. Did you have a higher score for Part 1 or Part 2? Read its description to learn what that means. Was the score tied? You use both emotion and logic to make decisions!

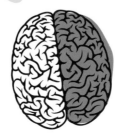

Part 1: You make decisions using emotions. You would be considered a right-brained thinker!

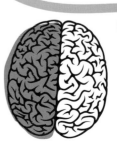

Part 2: You make decisions using logic. This means you are more of a left-brained person!

Chapter 7

KNOW YOUR BRAIN!

Both of your brain's hemispheres play an important role in the way you think, learn, and make decisions. But most people find they relate more to the functions of one hemisphere than the other. Even if you decide you are neither, using this theory is a great way to discover more about you!

KEEP EXPLORING!

The left-brain, right-brain theory is just one way you can get to know your brain. Other forms of self-discovery include dream interpretation, personality tests, and more. Use these fun methods to find out what makes you who you are. Soon, you will be an expert on you!

Brain Illusion Game!

Create a cool visual game that forces players to shift between using their left brain and right brain!

Materials:

- sheet of paper
- black marker
- notebook
- pencil

Test Yourself

- Look at this image. - - - - - - - - - -
- Do you see a vase or two faces? What you see first will depend on which side of your brain you use. Left-brained people see the vase first. Right-brained people see the faces.
- Look at the image again. Try to focus on the image that you did not see first. Write down whether this is difficult or not.
- Use your finger to trace the lines between the images.
- Step back and focus on the image you saw first. Is it hard to see this image again? Take note of how difficult this is for you.

Test Others

- On a sheet of paper, draw the image on page 28 so it takes up the entire sheet. Make the faces black. Leave the vase white.

- Show friends and family the image. Ask them what image they see first. Record their answers.

- Ask them to focus on the image they did not see first Ask them how difficult this task is for them.

- Have them trace the lines between the images using their finger.

- Have them step back and look at the image again. This time, have them focus on the image they saw first. As they focus, ask them how difficult it is to see the first image again.

Think It Over!

Review the notes you took. This game forces players to shift between using their left brain and right brain. What was different for people who came out as left-brained compared to people who identified as right-brained?

GLOSSARY

activating: turning something on, or causing it to work

anatomy: the structure of a living thing

automatic: done without your thinking about it

brainstorming: working with others to think of ideas

creative: skillful at using your imagination and making new things

demonstration: the act of showing how something works

diagrams: graphic designs or drawings that explain something

evaluate: to decide the value of something using careful thought

fantasy: a story with magical or odd characters, places, or events

hypnotized: a state in which a person appears to be sleeping but can still see, hear, and respond to suggestions and questions

ignite: to set in motion

logical: consistent with a reasonable way of thinking

productive: accomplishing a large amount of work or producing good results

rational: logical and sensible, not emotional

routine: a regular sequence of actions or doing things

technical: having to do with science, engineering, or the industrial or mechanical arts

traits: qualities or characteristics

FURTHER INFORMATION

Abramovitz, Melissa. *Brain Science*. Minneapolis, MN: Essential Library, 2016.

Learn all about the brand-new technology scientists are using to understand how the brain works.

Gardner, Jane P. *Brain*. New York, NY: AV2 by Weigl, 2017.

Learn all about your amazing brain and how it functions.

Moore, Gareth. *It's Only Logical*. Minneapolis, MN: Hungry Tomato, 2016.

Are you ready for some brain benders? Challenge your mind with the puzzles and other activities in this cool book.

One Brain...Or Two?

https://faculty.washington.edu/chudler/split.html

Learn about how the left brain and the right brain control your body at this website created by a real neuroscientist!

Your Brain & Nervous System

http://kidshealth.org/en/kids/brain.html

You know your brain helps determine your personality, but how does it work? Find out at this website!

INDEX

Photo Acknowledgments

The images in this book are used with the permission of: Design elements and doodles © advent/Shutterstock.com, Artfury/Shutterstock.com, Christopher Hall/Shutterstock.com, Dn Br/Shutterstock.com, Fandorina Liza/Shutterstock.com, Fears/Shutterstock.com, ipayo/Shutterstock.com, IrinaKorsakova/Shutterstock.com, kostolom3000/Shutterstock.com, mhatzapa/Shutterstock.com, Mighty Media, Inc., Mjosedesign/Shutterstock.com, Natasha Pankina/Shutterstock.com, Nikolaeva/Shutterstock.com, Ron and Joe/Shutterstock.com, Sashatigar/Shutterstock.com, StockSmartStart/Shutterstock.com, Vector Tradition/Shutterstock.com, and whitemomo/Shutterstock.com; © Monkey Business Images/Shutterstock.com, pp. 1 (top), 4 (top); © Pressmaster/Shutterstock.com, p. 1 (bottom); knape/iStockphoto.com, p. 3; © dddb/iStockphoto.com, p. 4 (middle); © fotoinfot/Shutterstock.com, p. 4 (bottom); © FatCamera/iStockphoto.com, pp. 5 (bottom, left), 17 (top), 27 (bottom); © PeopleImages/iStockphoto.com, p. 5 (top); © DAbeygoda/Shutterstock.com, p. 5 (bottom, right); © LisovyFamily/Shutterstock.com, p. 7; © Rawpixel.com/Shutterstock.com, p. 8; © gradyreese/iStockphoto.com, p. 10 (left); © zhu difeng/Shutterstock.com, p. 10 (right); © Karen Struthers/Shutterstock.com, p. 12; © Africa Studio/Shutterstock.com, p. 13; © Sunny studio/Shutterstock.com, p. 14; © sampsyseeds/iStockphoto.com, p. 15; © Zaitsava Olga/Shutterstock.com, p. 17 (bottom); © asiseeit/iStockphoto.com, p. 18; © dolgachov/iStockphoto.com, p. 19; © Feverpitched/iStockphoto.com, p. 22; © Igor Bulgarin/Shutterstock.com, p. 23; © Odua Images/Shutterstock.com, p. 26; © Iakov Filimonov/Shutterstock.com, p. 27 (top); © imagewriter/Shutterstock.com, p. 28; © Lucky Business/Shutterstock.com, p. 29; © Olena Yakobchuk/Shutterstock.com, p. 31.

Front cover: © SensorSpot/iStockphoto.com (top, left); © Pressmaster/Shutterstock.com (top, right); © Monkey Business Images/Shutterstock.com (bottom, left); © knape/iStockphoto.com (bottom, right).

Back cover: © FatCamera/iStockphoto.com (top); © Odua Images/Shutterstock.com (middle); © asiseeit/iStockphoto.com (bottom).

GRAYSLAKE AREA PUBLIC LIBRARY
100 Library Lane
Grayslake, IL 60030